HAPPINESS PROJECT

A Quest for Happiness – How to be
Happy – Loving Yourself – Feeling Good -
Choosing Happiness
and
Living in the Present

Jenna James

CONTENTS

INTRODUCTION

Reading this book can't achieve happiness for you – it can only try to point you in the direction to follow if you wish to arrive at a state of happiness. You will have to do the work yourself, make it your continuing project and be prepared to make changes in your thinking and in your life.

We all have just the one life, and it might as well be spent in the happiest way possible. This life that we have is the real thing and not a rehearsal - it's show-time! We can't have a replay – so we should try to get it right, to create the life we want.

Of course, we can't be bursting with happiness all the time, we will all have sad times, bad times, losses to cope with and unfortunate occurrences.   Your project is to accomplish happiness as your usual state, the norm.

Happiness Project is written simply and sincerely to highlight some of the steps we can take to lead us to the best experience of life that we can have. We hope this will help you on your way.

CHAPTER 1
THE QUEST FOR HAPPINESS: A WONDERFUL AND EXCITING JOURNEY

If you ask around you will discover that one of the many things people desire in their life, one of the most important ones, aside from wealth and good health, is happiness.

After all, we all want to be happy. From the moment we

developed self-awareness as a child, we have always wanted something or someone who can make us happy. As we mature, we have dreams and goals in life that we want to achieve and once we do achieve this, it can make us happy.

Happiness means different things to different people. It is a state of emotional or mental well-being that is characterised by pleasant, even joyful emotions that everyone is hoping to achieve. It is something people strive to find and keep. Yet, happiness is short-lived. Once anxiety, sadness, discontent, loneliness, anger and frustration seep into your life – the state of happiness is gone. The once blissful feeling is instantly replaced with negative emotions.

If you ask the people around you to explain what makes them happy they will definitely be able to give many and varied causes for happiness, some of them quite surprising. However, having the people they love in their lives, being financially stable, enjoying a successful career or a thriving business, or enjoying good health are just some of the more common reasons why people are happy.

Yet, if you don't have these – can you still be happy?

Happiness is a journey and not a destination.

The quest for happiness is, in truth a wonderful and exciting journey of self-discovery. It is reaching a certain point in life where you can enjoy the blissful feeling, in spite of all the challenges you face. Ever since our youth, we have been conditioned to think that if we can only reach a certain destination, find that special person, or complete a challenging project – we will be happy. Yet, happiness is not a future event. It is not about the future. Happiness is NOW. It is living this moment. Finding happiness in who we are and what we do - that is the important target to aim for.

Because life is a series of changing patterns – you can expect that there will be instances when something, or someone, will rob us of our happiness. Things will not always happen according to our desires. The people closest to our hearts will disappoint us.

2

Problems and challenges will continue to haunt our lives. Thus, happiness is not constant.

You can only find true happiness when you decide to live each and every moment to the fullest. It is when you view every day of your life as a day of discovery for yourself and others. It is when you savour and enjoy the knowledge that happiness is now.

CHAPTER 2
ACCEPTING, LOVING AND BEING YOURSELF

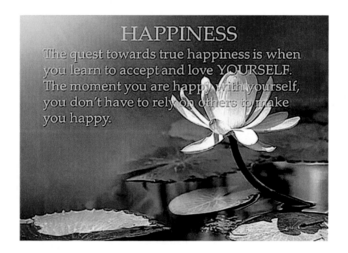

HAPPINESS

The quest towards true happiness is when you learn to accept and love YOURSELF. The moment you are happy with yourself, you don't have to rely on others to make you happy.

"Love is the master key that opens the gates of happiness."
~   Oliver Wendell Holmes

Love is the key to being happy in life.

Yet love should start within us. It is only when we learn how to accept,   love   and   be   ourselves,   are   we   able   to   truly   and unconditionally love others. Before we can even talk about loving others, it is important to focus on loving ourselves so that we are able to move forward in our quest for happiness.

How do you love yourself?

It is ironic that most of us find it easier to love others than to love ourselves. We can be kind to others, but we cannot be kind to ourselves. To learn how to love ourselves so that we can find true happiness, we have to start by taking care of our body, mind and spirit.
Body

How many times have we looked in the mirror and felt distaste and disappointment at what we see? We focus so much on the flaws that we hardly even notice the wonderful aspects of our physical body. When was the last time we really took notice of the depth of our eyes or the smiling lips that can light up our faces with beauty? We have to learn to love and accept our physical body – beauty, flaws and all.

Loving our body also means taking care of it. Opting for a healthy lifestyle – maintaining a proper diet, having a regular exercise regimen, refraining from smoking, minimising our alcohol intake and getting enough sleep are some of the best ways for us to have fit and healthy bodies. When we do this, we feel good about ourselves.

Mind

Our minds are very powerful. In fact, it is true that in life we don't always get what we want, but we get what we BELIEVE.

Loving ourselves means that it is essential that we nurture our minds with positivity. We need to surround ourselves with positive people. Focus on the positive events that occur. . The more we think positively, the more positive things happen. Positive things give us happiness - and it all starts with the mind.

Spirit

We can nurture our spirits with faith and hope in a Supreme Being. It is important that we learn to meditate regularly and get in touch with our inner being; at this time letting out all the toxic emotions that are clogging our quest for happiness.

We will find true happiness the moment we learn to accept ourselves. Accepting our self means knowing what makes us happy, or what makes us sad. It means knowing our dreams and accepting our failures. It means being bold enough to express our thoughts despite knowing that others will not be happy with our truthfulness.

It also means facing fear and never allowing it to stop us from achieving success.

Accepting who we are means boldly telling ourselves that, starting today, what other people say or think does not affect us any longer.

We must be ourselves. We don't have to follow what other people say that we must think and say. or how we act. We only have to follow what is in the heart.

We must celebrate who we are by loving, accepting and being ourselves, because we DESERVE it. No one will do a better job at loving yourself than YOU. Once you are able to do this -- you will then find happiness.

CHAPTER 3
BE KIND TO OTHERS

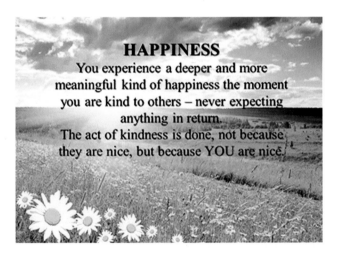

HAPPINESS
You experience a deeper and more meaningful kind of happiness the moment you are kind to others – never expecting anything in return.
The act of kindness is done, not because they are nice, but because YOU are nice.

"If you want others to be happy, practice compassion. If you want to be happy, practice compassion." ~ Dalai Lama

There is something beautiful and touching about being kind to others. Being kind means being compassionate. To be compassionate is to feel, to understand, and to show empathy towards other people and their suffering. It is letting other people know that you care.

Being compassionate to others does not mean being kind only to the people you know. Practicing goodwill to strangers and doing a random act of kindness will bring you happiness.

Being kind to others gives you a certain kind of happiness that is longer-lasting when compared with the level of happiness you can get when hanging out with friends, or buying the objects that you have always wanted. This happiness you feel is short-lived. The quest for true happiness is when you give yourself unselfishly to others without expecting anything in return.

Here are some steps on how to practice compassion:

Start by being kind to yourself.
Often times, people think that compassion is how you act towards others. But the truth is, you cannot practice compassion if you do not practice it within yourself.

It's difficult to be kind to others when you are struggling to be kind to yourself – when you are saying all those demeaning things like

"I'm not good enough"
"I'm a failure" or
"I'm so stupid".

Be kind to yourself by building yourself up. Think of all the good traits, the strong points in your character. Focus on these rather than the weaknesses.

Develop empathy for others.

Just like anything else, empathy can be developed. Deep inside almost all of us we have the ability to feel and understand what other people might be going through. However, it sort of gets lost along the way, especially if we focus too much on ourselves. We just have to practice empathy regularly to develop it.

How?

Think of anyone you know who is suffering. Imagine the pain and suffering they are going through. Try to feel it by putting yourself in their place. What would it take to ease the pain? You can also practice this towards people you don't know.

Find common ground with other people.

You can learn to be kind to others if you start looking for common ground with them.

Instead of thinking about how different they are from you, look for something that you find they have in common with you.

Here is an example:

My friend Julia and her husband had their house constructed, but they went over their budget. The worst thing happened after the house was finished - the couple found themselves almost bankrupt because Julia's husband was suddenly laid off work.

While Joe applied for other jobs, their only means to get by was going to their friends for financial assistance. It was a tough time for them. Even their friends had to make many excuses when they could no longer lend them money. It took them almost two years to recover. Joe got a job while Julia took on some freelancing jobs at home.

Because of their experience, they now understand how hard it is when you are placed in a financial bind without others to turn to. Thus, they now find it easier and want to help other people in need, as they once were.

"Like me, this person also wants to be happy "or
"Like me, this person is striving to meet his needs"

Once we are able to find common ground with other people, it is easier to be kind.

Remember that there is always something good in every person.

Many times, it is so difficult being nice to people who are unkind to you. It is natural that you will remember the occasions when they were mean. But once you focus on your decision to look at the overall goodness and worth of each person, it will change your perspective.

Showing kindness to others does not require reciprocation. If you are being kind AND waiting for them to acknowledge or reciprocate your kindness, you will just be frustrated.

Practice compassion and you will find true happiness.

CHAPTER 4
BE POSITIVE, BE HAPPY!

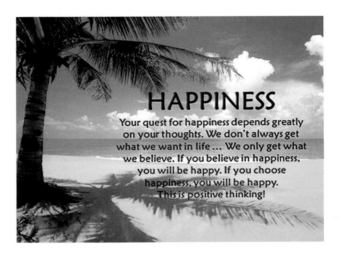

"It isn't what you have, or who you are, or where you are, or what you are doing that makes you happy or unhappy. It is what you think about." ~ Dale Carnegie

Without a doubt, our brain is very powerful, and it plays an extremely important role in our quest for happiness.

You must know that our brain monitors our thoughts and emotions to the point that any negativity that comes into our mind will cause it to create a feeling of sadness and stress to the body.

On the other hand, if the brain captures positive thoughts, it will give you a happy and a relaxed feeling. Thus, it is often said – to be happy, you have to choose to be happy. It simply means you will have to train your brain to think positively rather than dwelling on the negative.

Positive thinking is the key to making things happen. Many people become successful despite facing failures because they opt to think positively and believe that the more they try, the more they will reach success.

In just the same way, it is positive thinking that causes a person to be happy. If instead of focusing on the negative events that would usually cause unhappiness and discontent, you could choose to look for the positive aspects of your situation. This will improve your mood and bring you to a better disposition.

However, many would attest to the fact that choosing to think positively is not an easy feat, especially if all your life you have been used to thinking negatively.

All my life I have been filled with negativity. Every time I found myself in a tough situation, I would always think of the worst outcome so as to save myself from being disappointed or hurt. I used to feel that if I focused and hoped for a positive outcome, I would become frustrated because it would never happen for me. I felt that I might as well expect the worst.

At these times, I would endure so much anxiety and frustration that it prevented me from ever totally understanding the word "happy". Because of this attitude, I also attracted even more negative things to happen in my life. This of course caused me to become unhappy and insecure.

Overweight, financially strapped, with mounting debts and an ugly divorce, I decided things had to change.

... And the change should start with me and with my thoughts.

Steps to Think Positively and Cultivate Happiness:

Choose to be happy.

You have to believe that happiness is a choice. This also includes believing that you deserve all the happiness life can give. However, this isn't easy, since it is a natural tendency to blame outside forces like your parents, luck, fate, or relationships on why things don't work out as you wish. But no one is more in control of your thoughts than you are. It is always your choice to be happy.

Decide to get rid of negativity.

You will never be happy if you continue to live your life surrounded with negativity.

Negativity comes in different forms. The hype caused by the media about the perfect body or the perfect face will always affect how you see yourself. Negative people who constantly bombard you with toxic attitudes and views on life can certainly pull you down. Negative thoughts cannot coexist with positive ones. You have to decide, once and for all, to rid your life of all the negativity.

Opt to look at the positive side of every situation or person.

It is true that we have no control of other people or events in life, but we are in full control of our thoughts.

The moment you decide to be more positive, you will have to choose and focus on the positive side of every person and situation. If your boss gives you hell at work, focus on how he works hard to bring out the best in you. If your wife is nagging you to death, focus on how much she loves and cares for you and your children. If you find yourself having to forego some of the good things in life (like a vacation or a new car) because your finances are currently rocky, focus on how you are able to value and enjoy the simple things in life.

Reinforce and share positivity with others.

The very moment I decided that things in my life had to change, I started to learn how to think positively. Learning needs constant practice. It is not just in thoughts and in words, but in your actions too. It is also in sharing positivity with the people around you. The more you reinforce positivity in yourself and others, the more you are able to attract good vibes that give you a great sense of well-being.

"Think positively!" has been my mantra since then. Every time I talk to a friend and he starts dwelling on all the negative things happening in his life, I tell him to think positively and proceed to find positivity in his situation. Happily, it does soon influence him to view his current situation in a different light.

I came across a Hawaiian Shamanism teaching from Serge Kahili King, who said,

"We don't always get what we want in life … We only get what we BELIEVE."

It has changed how I view my life – from negativity towards positivity. Whatever you feel and believe, it will happen. If you believe that you deserve happiness, happiness will come. Believing is a reinforcement of positivity in your life. Get rid of the negative and start to think of the positive.

Your quest for happiness relies on your thoughts. Be positive. Be happy.

CHAPTER 5
IT'S YOUR CHOICE

Happiness is a Choice

It is your choice to be happy in whatever circumstances you are in. Happiness does not just happen in life. True happiness comes when you consciously choose it over the many challenges, unfortunate events and sadness that you face. Choose happiness today.

"Happiness is a choice. You can choose to be happy. There's going to be stress in life, but it's your choice whether you let it affect you or not." ~ Valerie Bertinelli

Being happy is a CHOICE.

Surprisingly, many of us have the wrong approach to the experience of happiness. We think that in order to be happy, we have first to be successful. We have to achieve something or have someone in our lives before we can experience true happiness. We believe that if we have plenty of money, if we have a wonderful career, or if we marry our dream girl/boy, we will be happy.

This is the wrong way of looking at it. It is like saying – the only time you will be considered a great athlete is when you win the race. The truth is, every athlete should be considered great, regardless of whether they win or lose, simply because of their hard work, persistence and sacrifices.

Some people think that happiness is a result of good luck or good fortune. It is a result of the right wheels turning at the right time. It is when you wake up in the morning, get up on the right side of the bed and then have everything working out just the way you want it to be. Yet, the truth of the matter is that happiness doesn't just happen. There will be good days AND bad days in life.

If you are happy in life, everything just follows. There is a domino effect to being happy. If you choose to be happy, you affect and influence the people around you and cause them to be happy themselves.

The environment in your household will be pleasant – making it a true haven to come home to. The stress which is often present in the work-place does not affect you too much because you and your colleagues are able to handle it. Despite the many challenges you face, you are able to take on life with good nature (which is a positive energy) causing positive things to happen.

Choosing happiness is not easy all the time.

This is quite true. After all, not everyone you meet will have a disposition similar to yours. There are often toxic people around you who may depress your spirits. You will find that on many occasions your hard work will not produce the results you want. Grief may strike, you may experience some tragic events. There may be days when you do not feel on top of the world. It is only human nature that you will feel inclined to withdraw, to stay in your unhappy corner. But, just like almost anything in life, happiness is a choice.

Once you choose happiness, despite your current circumstances, you will be amazed at how things will change from being negative to becoming positive!

Because we cannot stop unfortunate and undesirable events from happening, events that can rob us of our happiness, it is important that we should learn how to deal with these events.

As Dr. Daniel Friedland has said,
"The questions you are asking today will shape your destiny."

People who are happy are the ones who approach life's challenges with questions like ;

"What can I learn from this?" and
"What positive things can this challenge bring?"

They focus not on the circumstance, but on what really matters – the lessons they will learn and the possible outcome they want.

Once you consciously choose to be happy, you have to work on it.

You may not get it right at first, but as you continue your daily life with a positive attitude and the desire to focus on what life is teaching you, happiness comes more easily.

CHAPTER 6
THINGS YOU CAN DO TO BE HAPPY NOW

HAPPINESS

Your quest for happiness cannot be found in another place or another time.
Your happiness is here and it is now. It is in what you can do at this moment to make you happy.
If you want to be happy, choose to be happy because you know that
YOU DESERVE IT!

"I am determined to be cheerful and happy in whatever situation I may find myself. For I have learned that the greater part of our misery or unhappiness is determined not by our circumstance but by our disposition." ~ Martha Washington

Choose to be happy today.

I'm sure you want to be happy. There must be very, very few

people in the world, if any, who don't! The search for happiness can be a very real driving force in our lives. We can look for happiness in so many different ways and sometimes spend much time and effort in the search and never find more than a faint, fleeting reflection of it.

But the pursuit of happiness is simple. Unlike the popular notion that happiness is attained only if you are rich, successful or popular, happiness can be found in the simple things you can do now. Real happiness has nothing to do with money or status, you cannot buy it. It is a gift that you can give to yourself.

Realise and believe that happiness is yours.

You deserve to be happy. Happiness is not only for the rich and famous, or the successful people, but happiness is for you! This is the reason why you have to rid yourself of self-doubts and negativity. From now on, start each day with self-affirmation –

"I deserve happiness", or
"Happiness is mine".

Do something that you really enjoy.

Do you love dancing, singing, going to the movies, working in your garden, hiking, playing tennis, or going to the park and watching the sun set? Whatever it is, whatever raises your spirits, fills you with joy, set aside time to do it.

Take care of yourself.

How many times have we neglected ourselves? We spend time taking care of others when we should first take care of ourselves. Taking care of ourselves means taking care of our body, mind and soul. We should be enhancing and boosting our physical, mental and emotional well-being.

Give yourself small treats – because you deserve them!

When things go wrong (as they always will), don't give up – look for solutions.

Remember that life can be composed of good, bad and neutral . We need to learn how to deal with all three. We can do this by adjusting our attitude, looking for solutions and sometimes accepting with good grace what can't be changed.

Let go of your anger.

When people disappoint you or make you angry, do something thoughtful for them.

You are doing this, not for them, but for yourself. Letting go of anger and learning how to forgive will allow you to find true happiness.

Forget the past – it is done.

Move forward into the future with hope, faith and gratitude.

Do not allow yourself to get into a rut.

You have to challenge yourself, get out of your comfort zone, and try new things.

Spend more time with happy people.

Avoid the toxic ones.

Live in the moment.

I love the quote by Walt Whitman,

"Happiness – not in another place, but this place; Not in another hour, but this hour."

If you are looking for happiness, you will never find it in another place or another time. Happiness is where you are at the moment, right this minute

Don't stress over unimportant details in life.

Don't sweat over the small stuff. It will certainly lessen the stress level in your life if you can follow this advice.

Meditate daily

Clear your mind of all the negative emotions and thoughts. Allow yourself to relax in peace and the gratitude of simply being alive!

Be kind to others

Not just towards the people you know, but to strangers and also towards the most undeserving and undesirable individuals.

Give and receive love freely.

We are in this world to give and receive love . Without love, we will not be happy.

Laugh

To be able to find humour in many situations makes you a winner in life. Happiness can be found in simple, everyday living. It is how you perceive every event, every circumstance and every challenge. It is this that makes the difference.

We need to learn from little children. Look at their happy dispositions. They can find happiness in simple things. They have not yet learnt to complicate their lives. They have so much zest for life!

Most of all, to be happy is to learn how to be thankful.

Being grateful is not only for when things are working well in our lives, but it also means being thankful for the many trials and challenges we face that make us better people.

Our quest for happiness need not be complicated or difficult.

You can be happy now, if you choose it.

Your happiness is in your own hands.

AUTHOR'S NOTE

Recommended Book on this Subject

I hope you enjoyed 'Happiness Project'. If you would like to make any comments I would appreciate your review on:

http://www.amazon.com/dp/B00E8KKEJ0

Thank you for reading my book.

If you would like to read further on this subject I would recommend an excellent book by Karl Moore:

The 18 Rules of Happiness

http://www.amazon.com/dp/B004YOUPXY

Website

I hope you will visit my website for more information and videos about my books.

Please don't forget to sign up there for my Reader's Group so that I can send you a gift and occasional news about new books and special promotions. Thank you.

Http://www.evangeline.me

WITH SPECIAL THANKS

TO

CHARLENE

KINDLE BOOKS WHICH MAY INTEREST YOU

On Safari – Interactive Quiz Game by Evangeline Auld
http://www.amazon.com/dp/B0078DIGSA

How to Save Money - by Evangeline Auld
http://www.amazon.com/dp/B005JFBUYG

Dare to Date! – Advice on Dating by Lee and Jenna James
http://www.amazon.com/dp/B006T0DX68

House Sitting in France by Hilary Chase
http://www.amazon.com/dp/B004PLO61E

Heritage Sight – Satirical poem by Evangeline Auld
http://www.amazon.com/dp/B006HHVFAY

Curious Creatures – Animal verses by Evangeeline Auld -
illustrated
http://www.amazon.com/dp/B007PQV8GC

Clutter – Decluttering your Home – by Amy Younghusband
http://www.amazon.com/dp/B007JCGKQA

3 Day Nightmare – Thriller
http://www.amazon.com/dp/B0080Z7L40

Intrigue in Egypt – Romance/Thriller by Hilary Chase

http://www.amazon.com/dp/B008AMCW3S

60 Simple Recipes by Amy Younghusband
http://www.amazon.com/dp/B00998TNCU

Dilemma in Durban – Romance by Hilary Chase
http://www.amazon.com/dp/NWAWEK
The Parliament of Fowls – Chaucer, in modern English by
Evangeline Auld http://www.amazon.com/dp/B00A1HG66Y

Cat Burglar in Soho – Detective mystery Vol. 1 by Evangeline
Auld
http://www.amazon.com/dp/B00B0IBXBQ

Cat Burglar in Soho – Detective Mystery Vol. 1   - Paperback
http://www.amazon.com/dp/B00IHVR0H0

Cat Burglar in Mayfair – Detective mystery Vol. 2 by Evangeline
Auld
http://www.amazon.com/dp/B00BNMXX8K

Here be Dragons – Humorous verses on St George and the
Dragon
by Evangeline Auld
http://www.amazon.com/dp/B00BSY1ZZ6

The Cat who was Mad about Cheese verses for children
by Evangeline Auld
http://www.amazon.com/dp/B00CKBX9U0

Perverse Parodies - verses for grown-ups. By Evangeline Auld
http://www.amazon.com/dp/B00CLIKNWE

The Ballad of Jack Canvas – verse story for children (and perhaps
adults) – by Evangeline Auld
http://www.amazon.com/dp/B007GDV3IW

Gatsby the Great – children's book – by Evangeline Auld
http://www.amazon.com/dp/B00HHH2PUM

El Gran Gatsby – Spanish version of the above book
http://www.amazon.com/dp/B00K2ZBQMY

Protect Your Allergic Child – by Jenna James
http://www.amazon.com/dp/B00K5WJIVU

Allergies and You – by Jenna James
http://www.amazon.com/dp/B00K5WC6GE

Seven Little Fables by Evangeline Auld – Collection of 7 little
children's books, also available separately. (see below)
All stories to entertain and with a moral.
Proceeds all to Compass Children's Charity
http://www.amazon.com/dp/B00PHIOZDI

The Rooster and the Spotted Pig
Elephant and Butterfly
Little Green Frog and the Swan
Tortoise and Peacock
The Sloth and the Bee
Billygoat and the Crow
The Cat and the Squirrel

Chaos on Kariba – Drama and Romance by Hilary Chase
http://www.amazon.com/dp/B00UO7WOJY

Kindness Code by Jenna James
http://www.amazon.com/dp/B0149LUKPK

Unmasked by Hilary Chase - Cozy mystery No 1 in Elise Hagen
series
http://www.amazon.com/dp/B014JREO88

Last Gamble by Hilary Chase – Cozy mystery No 2 in Elise Hagen
series
http://www.amazon.com/dp/B016NEHL4E
Call of the Wild by Evangeline Auld – children's book
http://www.amazon.com/dp/B017ZZZAO8

Made in the USA
Lexington, KY
25 June 2018